Written by Sandy Ransford
Designed by Charlie Webster

First published in 1996 by HarperCollins Children's Books,
A Division of HarperCollins Publishers Ltd,
77-85 Fulham Palace Road,
London W6 8JB

Copyright © HarperCollins Publishers Ltd 1996

ISBN: 0 00 197913 2

Illustrations: Charlotte Hard
Photographs: Animals Unlimited: front cover top;
Aquila: /R Maier 7;
Bruce Coleman Limited: /F Prenzel 9;
Horizon: /H Ecker front cover main image;
Kit Houghton: 17b, 19, 20t, 20b, 29, 43, 50;
Jacana: /Axel cover spine, /J Ferrero 8b, 10, 13b, 24, /F Gohier
59t, / J Labat back cover, /E Pott 56;
Bob Langrish: 5, 14, 15, 21, 22t, 22b, 23, 25, 26, 27, 28, 30, 32t, 32b,
33, 34, 35, 36, 37, 38t, 38b, 40t, 40b, 41, 42, 44t, 44b, 45, 46, 47, 48,
49t, 49b, 51, 52, 53, 55, 58t, 59b;
Only Horses Picture Agency: 8t, 13t, 31, 54, 57, 58b;
Spectrum Colour Library: 17t, 18

A CIP record for this book is available from the British Library

Printed and bound in Hong Kong

Horses and Ponies

Collins *Children's* Books

CONTENTS

INTRODUCTION

 People first domesticated horses thousands of years ago. They bred strong horses to pull anything from a plough to a royal coach. They bred tough pack ponies to carry heavy loads. Huntsmen rode out on fast agile horses to catch animals for food and soldiers went into battle on sturdy chargers.

Today most
horses are
used for
pleasure but
there are many
different
breeds – each
one originally developed for a
specific task. In this book they are
divided into four sections: heavy
horses, middleweight horses, light
horses and ponies.

HORSE JARGON

Horses and ponies are measured in 'hands' from the ground to the withers, a hand being 10cm. A pony must be less than 14.2 hands high (hh), while a horse is anything taller.

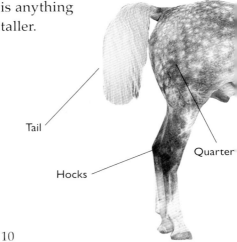

Tail

Quarter

Hocks

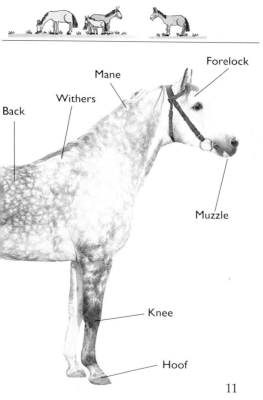

Forelock

Mane

Withers

Back

Muzzle

Knee

Hoof

11

SHIRE

The Shire is descended from horses that carried knights into battle in the Middle Ages. In Elizabethan times it was called the Great Horse of England. It is still Britain's largest workhorse, weighing over a tonne. It often has heavy white 'feather' round the feet. It is strong, docile and full of stamina, making it an ideal working horse. Some breweries use Shires as delivery horses.

Shires ploughing

At full
gallop

CLYDESDALE

The Clydesdale was produced in
Scotland in the 18th century by
crossing native breeds with
imported Flemish horses.
It is smaller than the
Shire, has feather
on its feet and

usually has a white face.
Clydesdale horses used to work
on farms in Scotland and
northern England. They often
wore elaborate harnesses.

PERCHERON

The name Percheron comes from
the region of France where this
horse was bred. Local mares were
crossed with Arab stallions
brought back to
France in Crusader
times. Today it is
one of the most
popular heavy
horses. The
Percheron has a calm
obedient nature and has been
used as a war horse, coach
horse, gun horse and working
farm horse. Its qualities also
make it a good riding horse.

SUFFOLK PUNCH

The Suffolk Punch has been bred
in East Anglia for almost 500
years. It is a powerful horse and is
always chestnut in colour.

Ready for haymaking

The Suffolk does not have feather
round its feet, so it can pull a
plough even through heavy clay
soil. It is an excellent farm horse
because it is cheap to feed and has
a long working life.

18

CLEVELAND BAY

The Cleveland Bay has pulled royal coaches on state occasions since the 1700s. It has been bred in Yorkshire for centuries. Before the arrival of the railways it served as a packhorse in coal mining regions.

IRISH DRAUGHT

The Irish Draught has been an all-round farm horse in Ireland for centuries. Both the Irish Draught and the Cleveland can be crossed with Thoroughbreds (see pages 26–27) to produce fast strong hunting horses.

The Hanoverian is a large elegant horse, with some Arab ancestry (see pages 24–25). It does well in dressage and show jumping. The breed is descended from war horses that fought at the Battle of Poitiers in 732AD. It was a favourite of the British monarchy from the 17th–19th centuries.

HOLSTEINER

The Holsteiner is another old German breed dating back to the 14th century. Today it competes successfully in dressage, show jumping and three-day eventing.

Show jumping at the Olympic Games

ARAB

The Arab is the oldest breed of horse and is often considered to be the most beautiful. It was first bred by nomads living in the Arabian desert thousands of years ago. The Arab is small, fast, strong and good-natured. It can be recognised by its silky mane and forelock, high tail carriage and its graceful movements.

Arab horses can be crossed with English Thoroughbreds to produce Anglo-Arabs which are taller.

THOROUGHBRED

Early morning gallop

The English
Thoroughbred
is descended
from three
18th-century
Arab stallions.
All race-horses are
Thoroughbreds: they

26

can sprint at speeds of over 64 kilometres per hour. They also succeed in the show ring, in show jumping, dressage and three-day eventing.

AKHAL-TEKÉ

Akhal-Tekés are strong but lightly built horses. They are from Turkmenskaya in the former Soviet Union. Their glossy coats are either bay, grey or dun (a pale yellow). They may have distinctive black points – mane, tail and lower legs. The Queen and the Prime Minister of Britain have both been presented with Akhal-Tekés.

The Akhal-Teké
s often described
as having a noble
expression

APPALOOSA

Appaloosas were bred in the Palouse valley, Idaho, USA by the Nez Percé Native Americans. They needed a sturdy horse for hunting buffalo and defending their homeland.

Appaloosas have dark raised spots which are often chocolate coloured

Appaloosas can have three
types of marking: leopard – a
white coat with dark spots
all over; blanket – a white
coat which has dark spots
over the hindquarters; and
snowflake – a dark coat with
white spots all over.

PALOMINO

Palominos are a colour type, not a breed. Although they originated in the USA, they are now found in many countries. Ideally, their coats should be metallic gold; their manes and tails white. They must have dark eyes.

PINTO

The name Pinto comes
from Spanish for
'painted'.

These brown and white
or black and white horses
are another American colour
type. They were prized by the
Native Americans, and are now
becoming popular as riding
horses in Britain.

33

HACKNEY

The Hackney was bred from
working farm horses in
Norfolk and Cumbria. It is
now a spectacular driving
horse or pony seen mainly in
the show ring. The trotting
action of the Hackney is
natural and unique: it
raises its knees very high

before throwing its forelegs
forward with a brief pause, so
that it appears to 'fly' over the
ground.

A Hackney showing
the high-kneed trot

LIPIZZANER

The Lipizzaner Stud was founded in the Austro-Hungarian Empire in 1580 and still supplies stallions to the famous Spanish Riding School in Vienna. These white horses are taught elegant movements called 'high school airs' which they perform worldwide.

Lipizzaners can be trained to perform remarkable feats

Lipizzaners are intelligent and docile, making them suitable as both riding and carriage horses. They can live to be 30 years old.

STANDARDBRED

The Standardbred is America's harness racing horse.

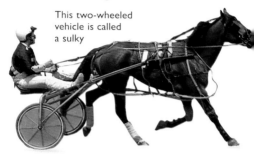

This two-wheeled vehicle is called a sulky

In this sport, competition rules
allow two types of leg
movement known as trotting
or pacing. For trotting the
speed record over one mile
(1.6km) is 1 minute 52.2
seconds and for pacing the
fastest ever horse has covered
the same distance in 1 minute
48.4 seconds.

AMERICAN QUARTER

The American Quarter Horse has been bred in the USA since the early 17th century for quarter-mile (0.4km) racing. They are powerfully-built, quick starters and fast sprinters. Off the racetrack, Quarter Horses are also valued by cattle ranchers because they are agile and even-tempered.

MORGAN

All Morgan horses can be traced back to one American stallion foaled in the 1790s called Justin Morgan.

A well-groomed Morgan

WALER

Horses arrived in Australia in 1795 and the name 'Waler' comes from New South Wales. Walers were used to herd sheep and cattle on the vast Australian ranges. In the 19th century they were exported to India as cavalry horses and were later supplied to the Allies during the First World War.

The Waler is a hardy horse and is
suited to a working farm life

They are good
jumpers – one
was said to have
cleared 2.54m in
the 1940s. They
can also perform
stunts at rodeos.

DARTMOOR

Dartmoor ponies have roamed wild on the rugged moorland in south-west England for centuries.

They are small, strong, tough ponies that can exist on poor fodder and withstand harsh winter weather.

EXMOOR

Exmoors are Britain's oldest breed of pony and have changed little from their prehistoric ancestors. Their thick double coats and distinctive hooded eyes protect them from extreme weather.

CONNEMARA

Connemaras may have existed in Ireland as far back as the 7th century BC. Invaders and traders then introduced Spanish horses, gradually modifying the Connemara breed.

They show great endurance and can find their way sure-footedly through bogs and boulders.

NEW FOREST

The New Forest is the second
largest of Britain's mountain and
moorland ponies.

Dun coloured
New Forest
pony with
white socks

New Forest ponies are hardy
enough to cope with their
heathland home and have also
become used to traffic and tourists.
They make ideal family ponies.

47

DALES

With their strong build, Dales ponies were used for carrying lead in mining areas east of the Pennines. They are still valued by hill farmers of this region, both as a driving pony and for herding sheep.

FELL

The Fell was a working farm and pack pony west of the Pennines. It is slightly smaller than its Dales cousin.

Fells are extremely hardy and sure-footed, making them ideal ponies for riding and driving in hilly countryside.

49

Highlands are the largest and
strongest of Britain's native
ponies. They were bred on the
Scottish Islands and mainland

where they were used for farming and deer-stalking. Today they make good trekking ponies because they are strong, docile and sure-footed. Highland ponies

often have a dark 'eel' stripe running along their backs.

There are four breeds of pony which are native to Wales. The Welsh Mountain pony looks like a miniature Arab and is probably the most beautiful. The Welsh pony and Cob Type are both slightly taller than the Welsh Mountain pony and the largest of the four breeds is the Welsh Cob. The Welsh Cob was developed for farm work and army duties.

Wels
Mounta
fo

HAFLINGER

The Haflinger is named after an Austrian village where it has worked for centuries as a pack and farm pony. It is very hardy and can carry heavy loads. In winter the Haflinger is also used to draw sleighs across the Alpine snow.

With its attractive chestnut colouring and flaxen mane, the Haflinger is gaining increasing popularity in Britain.

Haflingers have a natural elegance which makes them successful show ponies

ICELANDIC

Ponies were brought to Iceland from Norway and the Western Isles of Scotland in the 9th century. They were the Icelandic people's only means of transport for over 1,000 years. Icelandic ponies are small, stocky and immensely tough, with thick heavy manes. They carried people and goods safely across Iceland's frozen and rugged terrain. Today tourists visiting Iceland find pony-trekking the best way of exploring the spectacular scenery.

SHETLAND

The Shetland is Britain's smallest native pony. It is measured in centimetres rather than hands because it is so short. In spite of their size, Shetlands are tough powerful ponies and are full of character.

FALABELLA

The Falabella family from Buenos Aires in Argentina deliberately created this tiny breed which is closer to a miniature horse than a pony. Falabellas are the world's smallest horses. The shortest Falabella ever was a mare just 38cm high, weighing 12kg.

INDEX

Shetland 107CM	58	Thoroughbred 15–16.3HH	26–27
Shire 17HH	12–13	Waler 15–16HH	42–43
Standardbred 15.2HH	38–39	Welsh 12–15HH	52–53
Suffolk Punch 16HH	18–19		

HEIGHT CHART

Most horses and ponies are measured in hands. A hand is 10CM. Ponies are under 14.2HH (hands high) and horses are always over 14.2HH. Falabellas and Shetland ponies are measured in centimetres because they are so tiny.

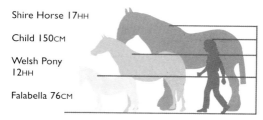

Shire Horse 17HH

Child 150CM

Welsh Pony 12HH

Falabella 76CM